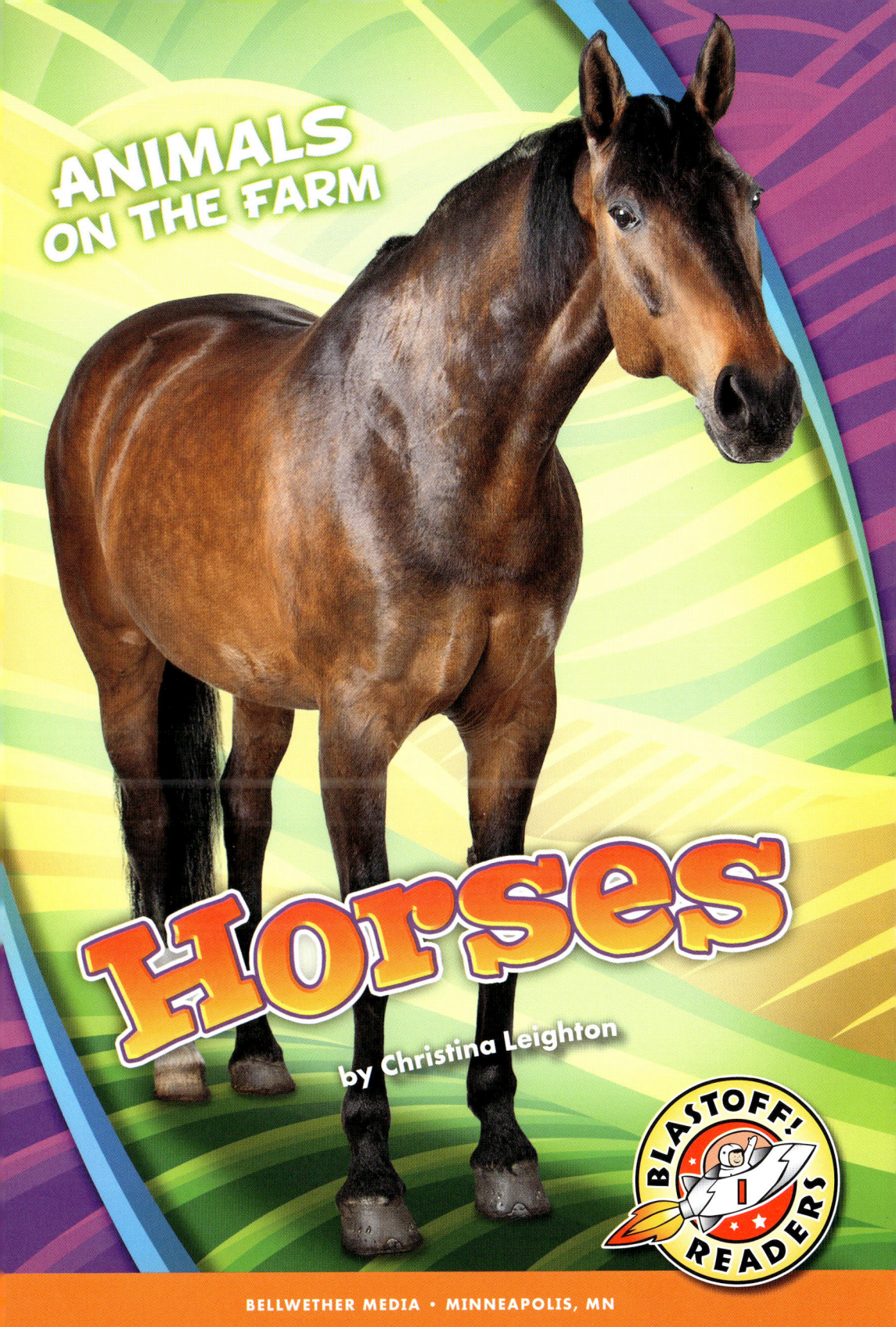

ANIMALS
ON THE FARM

Horses

by Christina Leighton

BELLWETHER MEDIA • MINNEAPOLIS, MN

BLASTOFF!
READERS

Note to Librarians, Teachers, and Parents:

Blastoff! Readers are carefully developed by literacy experts and combine standards-based content with developmentally appropriate text.

Level 1 provides the most support through repetition of high-frequency words, light text, predictable sentence patterns, and strong visual support.

Level 2 offers early readers a bit more challenge through varied simple sentences, increased text load, and less repetition of high-frequency words.

Level 3 advances early-fluent readers toward fluency through increased text and concept load, less reliance on visuals, longer sentences, and more literary language.

Level 4 builds reading stamina by providing more text per page, increased use of punctuation, greater variation in sentence patterns, and increasingly challenging vocabulary.

Level 5 encourages children to move from "learning to read" to "reading to learn" by providing even more text, varied writing styles, and less familiar topics.

Whichever book is right for your reader, Blastoff! Readers are the perfect books to build confidence and encourage a love of reading that will last a lifetime!

This edition first published in 2018 by Bellwether Media, Inc.

No part of this publication may be reproduced in whole or in part without written permission of the publisher. For information regarding permission, write to Bellwether Media, Inc., Attention: Permissions Department, 5357 Penn Avenue South, Minneapolis, MN 55419.

Library of Congress Cataloging-in-Publication Data

Names: Leighton, Christina, author.
Title: Horses / by Christina Leighton.
Description: Minneapolis, MN : Bellwether Media, Inc., 2018. | Series: Blastoff! Readers. Animals on the Farm | Includes bibliographical references and index. | Audience: Ages 5 to 8. | Audience: K to Grade 3.
Identifiers: LCCN 2017029537 | ISBN 9781626177246 (hardcover : alk. paper) | ISBN 9781681035048 (ebook)
Subjects: LCSH: Horses–Juvenile literature.
Classification: LCC SF302 .L45 2018 | DDC 636.1–dc23
LC record available at https://lccn.loc.gov/2017029537

Editor: Rebecca Sabelko   Designer: Lois Stanfield

Printed in the United States of America, North Mankato, MN.

Table of Contents

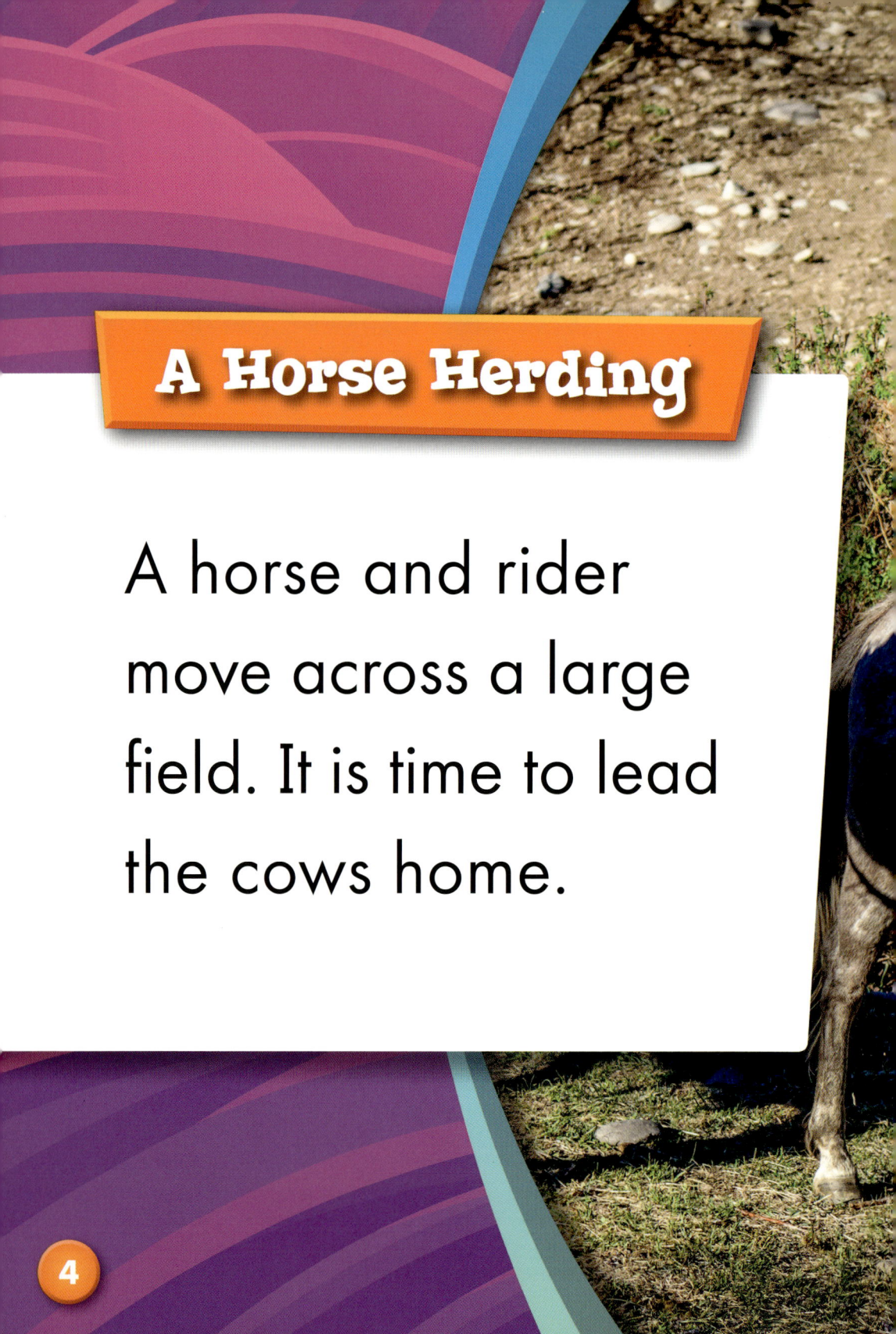

A Horse Herding

A horse and rider move across a large field. It is time to lead the cows home.

The team **herds** the cows into a pen. Good work!

What Are Horses?

Horses are strong **mammals** with long legs. They have short hair that shines in the sun.

NAMES:

males: stallions
females: mares
babies: foals

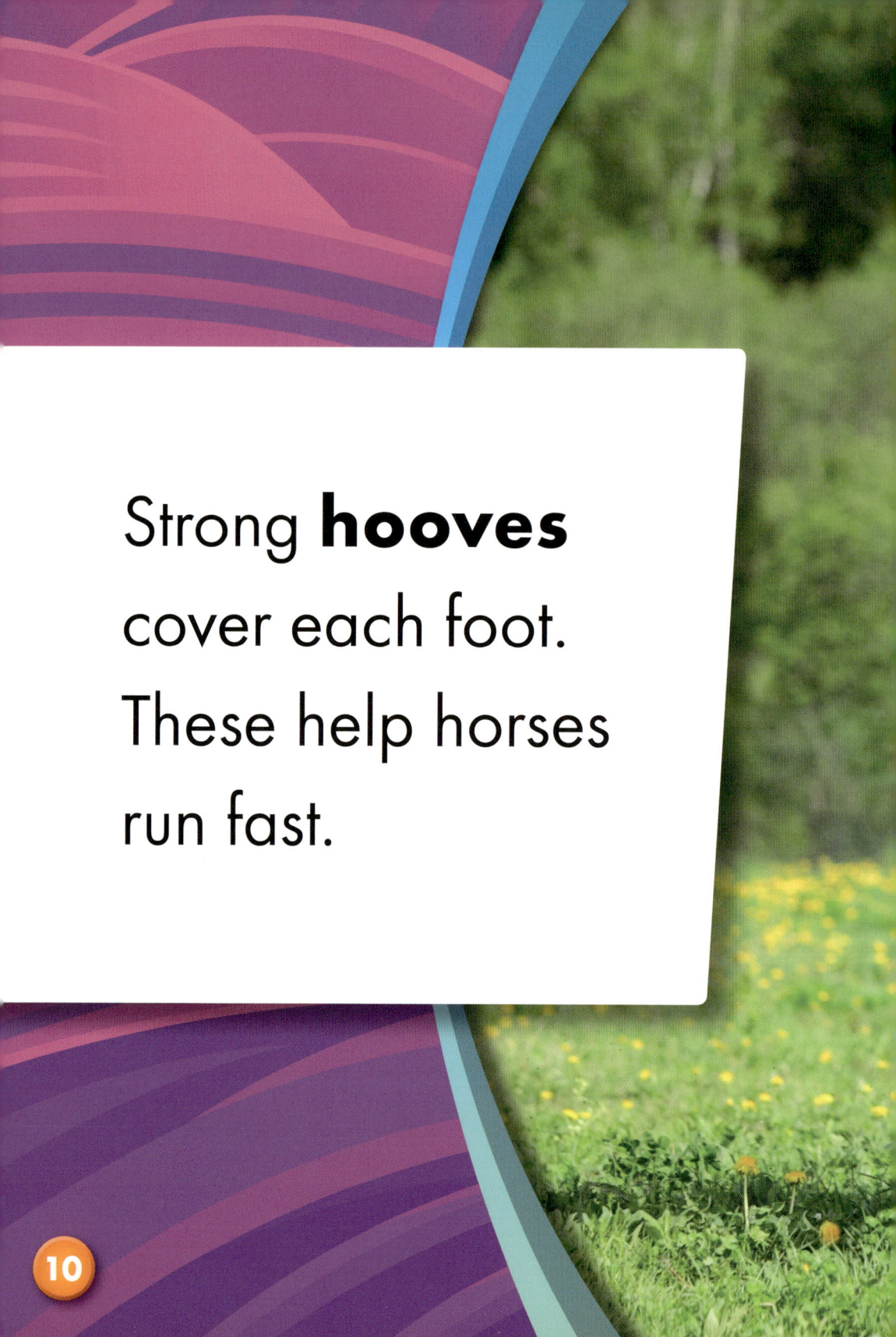

Strong **hooves** cover each foot. These help horses run fast.

hooves

Horses have big eyes and pointed ears. They can see and hear in all directions.

They have thick **manes** and tails. Their tails swish flies away.

mane

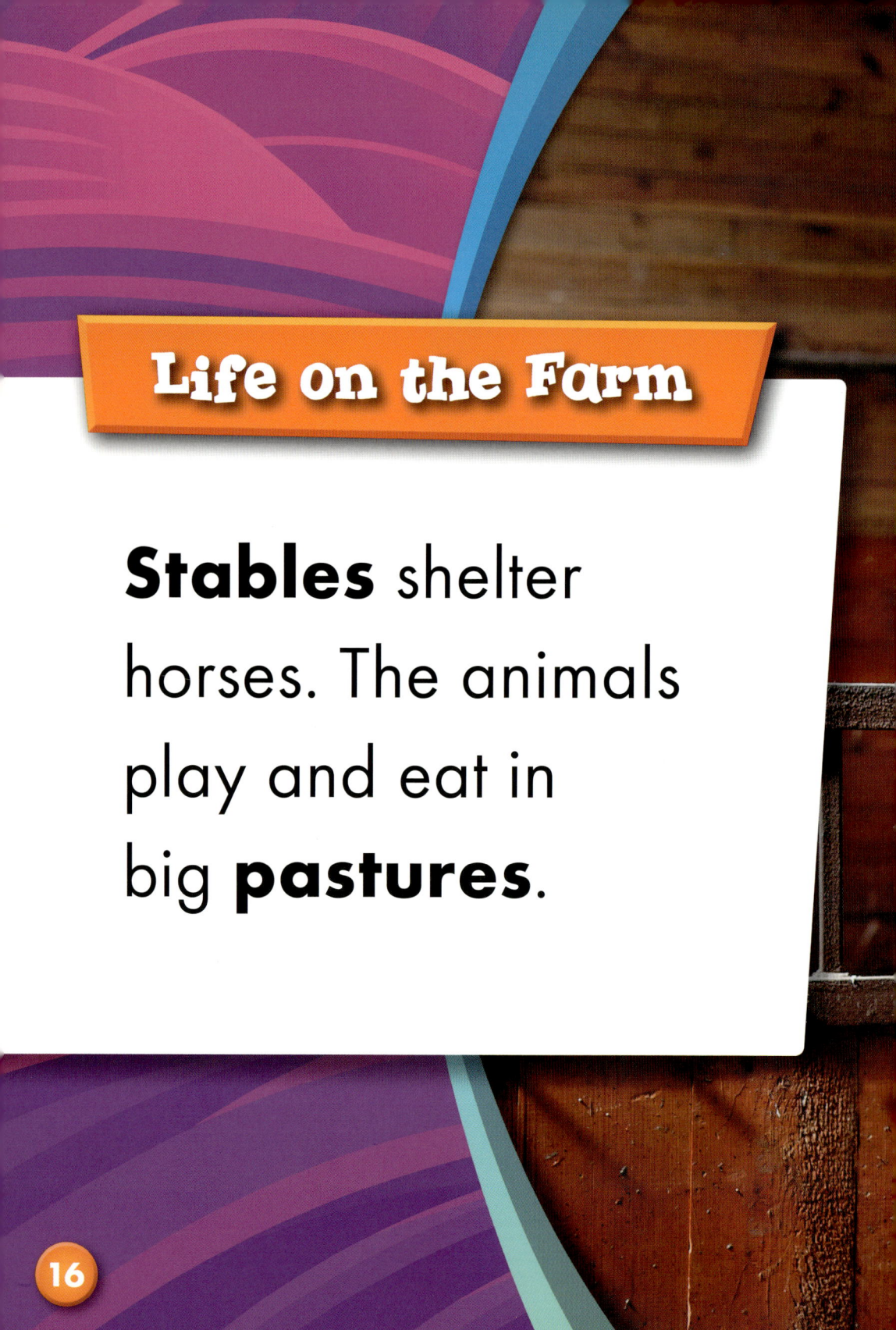

Stables shelter horses. The animals play and eat in big **pastures**.

stable

Horses eat hay and grass. Apples are a sweet treat.

FAVORITE FOODS:
grass, hay, oats

19

Many kinds of
horses live on farms.
These hard workers
are also loving pets!

neigh

Glossary

herds

controls the movements of animals

manes

long, flowing hair on the necks of horses

hooves

hard coverings on the feet of horses

pastures

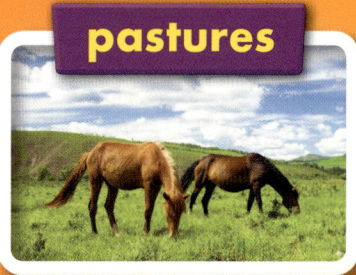

large fields where horses can feed on grasses and play

mammals

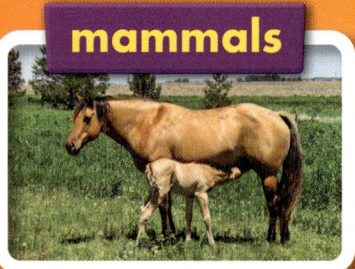

warm-blooded animals that have hair and feed their young milk

stables

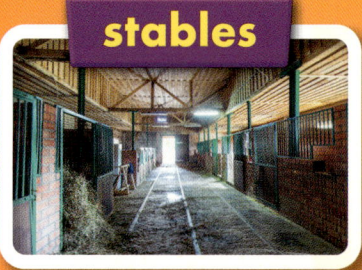

buildings with stalls where horses live

To Learn More

AT THE LIBRARY

Black, Vanessa. *Horses*. Minneapolis, Minn.: Jump!, 2017.

Hansen, Grace. *Clydesdale Horses*. Minneapolis, Minn.: ABDO Kids, 2017.

Olson, Bethany. *Baby Horses*. Minneapolis, Minn.: Bellwether Media, 2014.

ON THE WEB

Learning more about horses is as easy as 1, 2, 3.

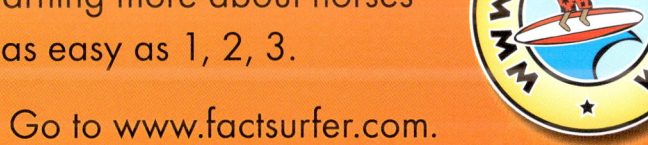

1. Go to www.factsurfer.com.

2. Enter "horses" into the search box.

3. Click the "Surf" button and you will see a list of related web sites.

With factsurfer.com, finding more information is just a click away.

Index